THE OFFICIAL  PET GUIDE

Care for Your

Budgerigar

CONTENTS

HarperCollins*Publishers*

First published in 1980 by
William Collins Sons & Co Ltd, London
New edition published in 1990

Reprinted by
HarperCollins*Publishers*
77-85 Fulham Palace Road
Hammersmith
London W6 8JB

The HarperCollins website address is
www.**fire**and**water**.com

07 06 05 04 03 02
16 15 14 13 12

This is a fully revised and extended edition of *Care for your Budgerigar*, first
published in 1980 and reprinted 11 times

Text of the 1980 edition by Tina Hearne; text revisions and additions for
this edition by Michael Pollard

Designed and edited by The Templar Company plc
Pippbrook Mill, London Road, Dorking, Surrey RH4 1JE

Front cover photograph: Animal Ark, London
Text photographs: Animal Photography Ltd, Dennis Avon,
Bruce Coleman Ltd *(also back cover, bottom)*, Robert Estall,
Marc Henrie, Arthur Hissey, Eric Hosking, Frank W. Lane,
C & L Nature (Cyril Laubscher), Pedigree Pet Foods Education Centre,
Photo Library International, Spectrum, ZEFA

Illustrations: Tony Morris and Bob Hersey/Bernard Thornton Artists

**A catalogue record for this book is available
from the British Library**

ISBN 0 00 412544 4

Printed by Midas Printing Ltd, Hong Kong

First things first, animals are fun. Anybody who has ever enjoyed the company of a pet knows well enough just how strong the bond between human and animal can be. Elderly or lonely people often depend on a pet for their only company, and this can be a rewarding relationship for both human and animal. Doctors have proved that animals can be instrumental in the prevention of and recovery from mental or physical disease. Children learn the meaning of loyalty, unselfishness and friendship by growing up with animals.

But the commitment to an animal doesn't begin and end with a visit to the local pet shop. A pet should never be given as a 'surprise' present. The decision to bring a pet into your home should always be discussed and agreed by all the members of your family. Bear in mind that parents are ultimately responsible for the health and well-being of the animal for the whole of its lifetime. If you are not prepared for the inevitable expense, time, patience and occasional frustration involved, then the RSPCA would much rather that you didn't have a pet.

Armed with the facts, aware of the pitfalls but still confident of your ability to give a pet a good home, the next step is to find where you can get an animal from. Seek the advice of a veterinary surgeon or RSPCA Inspector about reputable local breeders or suppliers. Do consider the possibility of offering a home to an animal from an RSPCA establishment. There are no animals more deserving of loving owners.

As for the care of your pet, you should find in this book all you need to know to keep it happy, healthy and rewarding for many years to come. Responsible ownership means happy pets. Enjoy the experience!

Terence C. Bate

TERENCE BATE BVSc, LLB, MRCVS
Chief Veterinary Officer, RSPCA

Introduction

The budgerigar is a small species of parrot, native to Australia, where it roves over the semi-arid interior plains in vast flocks. During the last century naturalists introduced the budgerigar into Europe, where its popularity was such that it was soon in great demand. Throughout the nineteenth century nets were laid out on their feeding grounds to catch the wild budgerigars as they came down for seeding grasses. Those which survived being netted were transported to Europe, where they were bred and have become the ancestors of the domestic budgerigar. All budgerigars now offered for sale have been bred in captivity.

Budgerigars do not build nests. In the wild they lay their eggs in any convenient place, such as a hollow tree, which affords protection and enables them to roll the eggs during the incubation period. Given suitable nesting-boxes in a breeding cage, budgerigars can be successfully bred in captivity.

Caged budgerigars are much less fortunate, but they are particularly good pets for a family with very limited space and possibly modest means. If possible, keep a pair of budgerigars in a good-sized cage. It is essential that caged birds be given daily exercise out of the cage. When a budgerigar has to be kept alone it will need the stimulation of appropriate toys, and plenty of human contact. Young budgerigars may learn to talk if they receive lots of encouragement before the age of six months.

Budgerigars are cheerful, hardy companions which respond well to training and companionship and develop distinctive characters. Just how much individuality they show depends, as with all pet animals, on the degree of freedom they are allowed, and on the stimulation provided by their surroundings and their companions. The only time fit budgerigars lack vitality is when they are moulting, which seems to be very debilitating for a short while.

The care of budgerigars could hardly be more simple, and it is not surprising that there are thought to be six million of these agreeable little birds in Britain alone.

Budgerigars in the Australian outback

The vast semi–arid grasslands of the Australian interior are the natural home of the budgerigar. It is a migratory bird, spending summer in the cooler south of the continent and flying north for the winter. Within this general annual pattern, however, flocks are constantly on the move, partly to find fresh sources of food and water and partly to avoid excessive heat. Unlike many other migratory birds such as swallows, budgerigars do not return to the same site every year. They are opportunistic rovers.

The typical vegetation of the budgerigar's favoured environment is scrub grass, which provides food when it seeds, and eucalyptus trees, which provide shelter and nesting places. Budgerigars' water requirement is relatively low, but a supply is, of course, essential. Their need to conserve water is reflected in the fact that they excrete very little, resulting in almost dry droppings.

The natural breeding season is from October to December. During the incubation period, the cock feeds the hen, and he helps with the feeding of the young by dehusking seeds for them. The learning phase of the young chick's life is very intense, and at six weeks it is fully fledged and ready to migrate with its parents.

Varieties

There are over 100 different colour varieties recognized by budgerigar breeders, all produced by selective breeding from mutants of the wild light green type. For owners who do not wish to breed from their birds, the choice of a particular colour is a matter of personal taste. The longevity or good health of the colour varieties does not differ significantly.

LIGHT GREEN
Wild budgerigars are generally light green, with a yellow mask, shoulders and wings. The six throat spots, the wing and head markings are black. The domestic Light Green variety is closest to the wild type, but larger.

Different colours such as light yellow or dark green appear from time to time in a wild flock, but the new sports, or mutations, tend to die out in the wild.

BASIC COLOUR SERIES
In captivity the mutant forms, when they occur, are 'fixed' by breeding the mutant back to its offspring. The four colour series are **Blue** and **White**, which have a white ground colour, and **Green** and **Yellow**, which have a yellow ground.

There are three shades of each colour. The three shades of the Blue series, illustrated left, are Sky Blue (light), Cobalt (medium) and Mauve (dark). The three Whites are White Sky Blue (light), White Cobalt (medium) and White Mauve (dark). In the Green series, the succession is, confusingly, Light Green (light), Dark Green (medium) and Olive Green (dark). The yellow follows this same classification.

COLOUR FACTORS
The basic colour series are modified by the Grey, Slate and Violet colour factors, which occur in the light, medium and dark shades. There are, for example, Grey Greens, Grey Dark Greens and Grey Olive Greens. The Slate factor also modifies the basic colours slightly. The Violet factor does

L Sky Blue   R Light Green cock

Cobalt cock

L Mauve cock   R Light Green hen

Green and Yellow cock

L Dark Green cock   R Lutino hen

Albino cock

not make a bird that colour, except in the Violet Cobalts, but it intensifies the colour.

ALBINOS AND LUTINOS
Albinos and Lutinos are mutations resulting from a lack of pigmentation. Blues and Whites, which have a white ground colour, produce Albinos. Mutation of the yellow ground colour of Greens and Yellows produces an entirely yellow bird, the Lutino. Both Albinos and Lutinos have red eyes.

PIED BUDGERIGARS
Pied varieties, sometimes called Variegated or Harlequin budgerigars, have broad bands or patches of a second colour over parts of the body. Frequently the upper chest is yellow, with a band of green below. In the Blue series, the chest is banded blue and white.

OPALINE BUDGERIGARS

Budgerigars with the standard pattern of markings are known as 'normal'. Opalines show variations of the standard pattern. Ideally, there are no head markings and the body colour and the ground colour of the wings correspond. The Opalines' most distinctive feature is a large 'V' of pure colour with no markings, called the mantle, between the wings.

CRESTED BUDGERIGARS

There are three types of crested budgerigars: those with a flat circular crest, like a Norwich canary; those with a half crest or fringe; and those with a tufted crest.

CINNAMONS AND GREYWINGS

Cinnamons and Greywings are bred from mutants with paler wing markings than the normal black. Cinnamons have a less intense body colour than normal, and the head and wing markings and throat spots are reduced to a light cinnamon brown. In Greywings, all the black markings are reduced to light grey and the body colour is also reduced.

L Pied Opaline Cobalt
R Grey Green

Grey cock with flat circular crest

Biology

Feathers Feathers provide a water-repellent insulation around the body, allowing the budgerigar to maintain a constant temperature. Different feathers, for instance the flights, and down, are adapted for specialized use, and all are attached to muscle for movement. When the feathers are fluffed out a greater volume of air is trapped close to the body for extra warmth. When they lie flat, this volume of air is reduced.

Budgerigars renew their feathers periodically by moulting. Frequent preening keeps the feathers in good condition, and completely restores the structure of those damaged when, as sometimes happens, the interlocking barbules are torn apart.

Temperature Birds are warm-blooded, or homoiothermic, with a constant body temperature. In the budgerigar this is between 40°C/104°F and 42°C/108°F. To retain body heat, the budgerigar fluffs out its feathers; to lose it, the bird increases its normal breathing rate above the normal 80–100 per minute, so that heat is lost through expired air. There are no sweat glands through which water may evaporate on the skin surface to reduce body temperature.

Shape The streamlined body shape of budgerigars and all birds is, biologically, a necessary adaptation for flight. Breeders value it for aesthetic reasons, and count all the following as faults for exhibition purposes: roach back, pronounced neck, pronounced chest, pronounced paunch, thinness, cross wing tips, protruding beak, and flattened head.

Interlocking barbules – magnified

Toes Instead of the typical arrangement of three toes forward, and one backward, the budgerigar's toes are paired. One pair is directed forward; the other backward. This is an aid to climbing and is seen in other climbing birds, notably the woodpeckers. The paired arrangement is known as 'zygodactyl', a word derived from the Greek *zygon*, meaning a yoke.

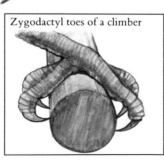

Zygodactyl toes of a climber

Vent The vent or cloaca, is a single opening which is common to the reproductive, digestive and excretory systems. The droppings are a combination of faeces and uric acid crystals, which quickly dry out. In general, birds excrete very little water. Budgerigars, in particular, having evolved in the semi-arid conditions of the Australian outback, do not waste water through excretion.

Cock's cere: blue Hen's cere: brown

Cere The cere is the exposed waxy membrane at the base of the beak which is coloured differently according to sex. The word, cere, is derived from the Latin *cera*, meaning wax.

Eyes Birds such as the budgerigar, with eyes set to the sides of the head, have very good sight compared with our own. Our field of vision extends over an angle of about 200°, but only 2° is in sharp focus. Not only is the budgerigar's field of vision much wider, but all the images received, no matter how obliquely, are in sharp focus.

The eyes are protected by three eyelids: the upper, the lower, and the nictitating membrane, which is vestigial in man. The budgerigar, however, can close the third eyelid across the front surface of the eyeball for cleaning, and for protection.

Beak A bird's beak is another adaptation to flight. Heavy jaws and teeth have been replaced by a beak of light-weight keratin. The variation in form is needed to suit very different modes of life and feeding.

This shape of beak is common to the parrot family, and is particularly well adapted for removing the husks from seed. It is also a considerable aid to climbing, and active budgerigars can often be seen using it as such.

Sometimes the beak is malformed at birth. When the upper mandible is overdeveloped, relative to the lower, the beak is known as 'overshot'. When the lower mandible is overdeveloped, the fault is known as 'undershot'. Veterinary advice should be sought.

Severely undershot beak

Wings The wings correspond to the fore limbs of other land vertebrates. The large surface area needed for successful adaptation to flight is provided by feathers. These, combined with a very light skeleton, give a big wing area with little increase in weight and minimum loss of body heat.

Choosing a budgerigar

Should someone new to budgerigars choose a male or female, a young or a more mature bird? Male budgerigars are more easily trained, and are the better choice unless the owner wants to breed. Young birds can be trained from about six weeks. Older birds may well have been trained, but if not they are unlikely to respond after the age of about six months.

WHERE TO BUY

A recognized breeder is the best source. Many breeders are happy to sell birds which are unsuitable for breeding or showing but are perfectly healthy and suitable as pets. It is better to buy from a large pet shop than from an unrecognized breeder. Birds should not be bought from such outlets as market stalls. See p.33 for information on how to identify a healthy budgerigar.

CHECKING SEX AND AGE

The cere (see p.13) is the key to a budgerigar's sex, but sexing a young bird is not easy and even experts can make mistakes. In a young male, the cere is pink, turning blue in maturity. The young female's cere is bluish-white and turns brown.

Age is more easily checked. Young birds have bars of colour from the cere to the forehead or 'cap'. These begin to disappear at three months, when the cere changes colour.

COMPANION BUDGERIGARS

As they are flock birds, budgerigars quickly become bored if they are left too much to themselves. Plenty of human contact, suitable toys and daily exercise will help, but the best way to keep a budgerigar interested is to provide a companion budgerigar. The two should be acquired at the same time and housed together to avoid jealousy. Two males or two females may be kept together. Two birds kept together cannot, however, be trained to talk as they do not bond sufficiently to their owner.

The sex of adult budgerigars is easily distinguished by the colour of their ceres – blue for cocks, brown for hens.

Budgerigars may be kept in an aviary with other birds such as cockatiels and the larger finches. Here, a budgerigar is joined by a cockatiel and a red canary. (Owners should be aware that smaller birds such as canaries are in danger of being bullied. A more suitable companion would be a large finch.)

Pied budgerigars *L.* to *R.* Pied White cock: Pied Green cock:
Pied Blue cock: Pied Cobalt cock

Opaline Cinnamon Sky Blue baby hen

Opaline Dark Green hen

Opaline Grey Green cock

Grey cock

Aviaries

A well-built aviary is the most satisfactory and attractive housing for budgerigars. They are able to live gregariously as in the wild, enjoying freedom of movement and some flight, albeit restricted. It also offers the best possible chance of observing their behaviour in captivity. An aviary also opens up the possibility of keeping compatible species together. Budgerigars must not be kept with small birds such as canaries, which they tend to bully, but other small members of the parrot family, such as the cockatiels, as well as weavers and zebra finches, are compatible.

BASIC DESIGN
Aviaries vary greatly in design, but the two essentials are an outdoor flight area and a weatherproof sleeping area. Budgerigars are extremely susceptible to draughts, and special care should be taken in the positioning and construction of the sleeping quarters to ensure that they are draughtproof, but at the same time ventilated.

CONSTRUCTION
The most usual construction is of timber, with wire mesh or weld mesh screens, and a double door for security. For preference, the aviary should be built on a concrete apron, or some similar hard-standing, which is easily sluiced down, and rat-proof. Even so, one has to remain vigilant since rats can climb the wire mesh and gain access through the eaves.

FAVOURED ASPECT
The aviary should be sited so that it catches the sun, preferably in the morning or evening rather than in the full heat of the day, but part of the flight area should offer shade and protection from the weather at all times.

FURNISHINGS
The sleeping area needs to be furnished with plenty of perching for the number of birds kept, preferably all of it at

Where space permits, an aviary will allow a number of birds to be kept in much more congenial living conditions than a cage, however roomy, can offer. It should be secure and include an outdoor flight area and sleeping quarters which protect the budgerigars both from the elements and from predators.

a uniform high level. The budgerigar's preference is always for height, and this will prevent jostling for more favoured positions. Perches should be in a variety of sizes and diameters so that birds do not get cramp from continually gripping identical perches.

Nesting boxes, when they are provided, may be hung in the enclosed area, or out in the flight space. Essentially, these are secure, dark boxes with popholes and a floor with a hollow in which the eggs will be laid (see p.40). Budgerigars require no nesting material, but a floor lining of sawdust may be provided and will aid cleaning.

The flight area will needs lots of perching, some under the protection of the main roof overhang, but not all. Budgerigars sometimes enjoy a soaking in the rain. There will also need to be a bird table for food pots. Other accessories, including the water pots, mineral licks, cuttlefish 'bone', swings, ladders and bunches of seeding grasses can be suspended from the mesh of the wall screens or roof.

Perching Plenty of perching places – far more than would seem strictly necessary for the number of birds kept – will be necessary to prevent jostling for favourite positions. We think of budgerigars as extremely docile, but they are capable of being pugnacious with their own kind on occasion. Their particular liking for height should be borne in mind when positioning both perching and nesting boxes.

Catching aviary birds Unless an owner spends a great deal of time with the birds, they are unlikely to allow themselves to be handled. Most aviary owners keep a long-handled net for catching their birds should the need arise.

Bird table Seed and water hoppers, sprays of seeding grasses and millet are best distributed throughout the aviary, and on the bird table. There will be squabbling unless the birds have room to feed without interference from others.

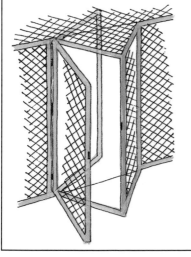

Double security doors The double doors are a necessary security device to prevent the budgerigars escaping. One door must always be shut before the other is opened, and there must be no space for the birds to fly over the inner door. In the main picture the inner door is placed across one corner, while the detail on the left illustrates an exterior 'porch'. In both, there is a ceiling over the triangle of space defined by the double doors.

Hatchway The budgerigars enter and leave the sleeping quarters by way of a hatch, which should be closed in the evening, when they are all roosting, and opened early in the morning.

Sleeping quarters Inside the sleeping quarters the budgerigars must have adequate perching in a dark, draughtproof area, ventilated by an adjustable grille. Budgerigars are hardy enough to withstand winter temperatures if their sleeping compartment is sturdily built and frost proof.

Roofing Height is important. Budgerigars like to be able to fly and to perch at a good height, and there should be adequate headroom for the keeper to work inside the aviary in comfort.

The sleeping compartment must be strongly roofed, together with the outside flight area, to give protection in bad weather.

Hard standing The aviary is most conveniently sited on hard standing, which should also be a deterrent to rats. Sometimes rats are attracted to an aviary both by the birds and by the presence of their food, and the best aviaries are constructed as rat-proof as possible. Since rats are capable of climbing the wire mesh screens of the flight area, it should not be possible for them to gain access easily at the level of the roof eaves.

Nesting boxes Nesting boxes may be provided in the spring either in the sleeping quarters or in the flight area. Provide more boxes than there are pairs of budgerigars, to allow for some choice of site, and position all the boxes at the same height. It is at breeding times that the birds may be quarrelsome, and an odd cock particularly so. An odd hen is unlikely to be difficult: almost certainly one of the cocks would raise two families simultaneously, but he would become exhausted doing so, and it is far better to keep an equal number of cocks and hens.

Caging

Housing budgerigars in a cage is much less satisfactory than in an aviary. As some recompense for cramped conditions the birds will need lots of human contact to which they respond with singing and talking. It is essential that they are allowed a period of free flight – exercise out of the cage – each day, preferably when they are most active, such as in the early morning.

CONSTRUCTION OF CAGE

Choose as large a cage as possible, suitable for housing two budgerigars, with enough room for them to move around it with ease. Manufactured cages are usually made of metal with wire mesh screening. The bars should lie horizontally, to provide a climbing frame.

A home-made budgerigar cage constructed of timber with a wire mesh or weld mesh front, like the breeding cage shown on p.41, has the advantage of being draught-proof and roomy, and devoid of gimmicky features.

Cages of these patterns are not recommended. The vertical bars of the cage on the left cannot be used for climbing and there are no perches. The cage on the right is far too narrow.

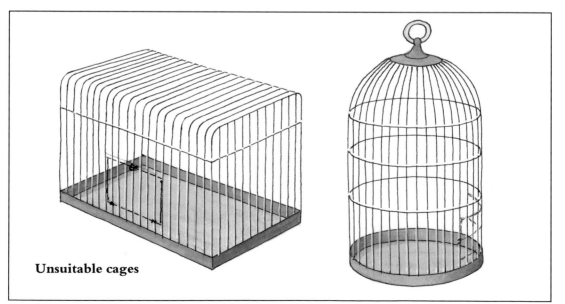

Unsuitable cages

POSITION OF CAGE

The cage should be positioned in a room where the birds will have human contact and yet can be allowed out of the cage in safety. Other pets and very young children should, of course, be excluded during free flight periods. Windows should be closed and fireplaces guarded even if there is no fire, and heaters or fans should be switched off. Some house plants are poisonous to budgerigars and they should be removed or covered. If the birds show any inclination to fly into the windows these should be screened with light coloured blinds or netting. Similarly, the door should be hung with a bead, bamboo or net curtain to form a barrier even when it is left open accidentally.

In many small households, where there is no danger of outside doors being left open, the birds can be left free all day to come and go into their cage as they will.

The cage should not stand in direct sunshine, or in a draught. Many owners find it best to hang the cage on a portable stand that can be repositioned at any time for the comfort of the budgerigar. Birds can be distressed by a smoky atmosphere, and if there are smokers in the house, or an open fire, it is wise to cover the cage and remove it to another room.

Budgerigars living indoors benefit from plenty of human companionship.

FURNISHING THE CAGE

The cage needs to be furnished with perches close to each food and water pot, with a high perch for use at all other times. Bought cages are equipped with dowling perches 1 cm/½ in diameter, which are much less satisfactory than a piece of fruit-tree branch which makes a good natural perch. Sand or sandpaper is usually used to line the base of the cage, and ladders, bells, ropes, swings and mirrors are all suitable toys, providing the cage is not over-furnished with them. Toys made of natural materials such as wood are to be preferred, as budgerigars tend to peck at toys, and there is a danger of plastic toys splintering. It adds interest to the budgerigar's life if toys are rotated so that each day or so a new object is presented to be explored and enjoyed.

A variety of carefully chosen toys and perches will help to ensure that caged budgerigars do not get bored.

Feeding and watering

SEED MIXTURE

In the wild, budgerigars feed on seeding grasses, which is why they must be fed mixed seed in captivity.

A variety of packeted seed mixes is available. Most are predominantly mixtures of canary seed and millet. The better mixtures are improved by the addition of red rape, linseed, or niger, which are particularly nutritious seeds, with a high fat and protein content. Some mixtures have artificial grains added, with additional nutrients.

Budgerigars also welcome some variety, in the form of sunflower seed and wheat germ, and it is a good practice to hang a bunch of seeding grasses for them.

The budgerigars eat only the kernel of the seed: the husks are always discarded. For this reason owners of caged birds should get into the habit of blowing away the husks that the birds deposit on top of their seed containers. It has been known for budgerigars to starve in a cage where seed was available, hidden by a layer of husks.

FRESH GREEN FOOD

In the wild, budgerigars eat fresh green food as well as seeding grasses. From time to time there are very severe thunderstorms in the Australian interior, and although the land is arid, after a downpour seeds germinate very quickly to produce a lush but short-lived pasture. Budgerigars alight on these pastures to take the green plants, and in captivity will eat chickweed, groundsel, dandelion, and salad greenstuff. Some birds also like a segment of apple or orange; others enjoy grated carrot.

millet spray

groundsel

chickweed

dandelion

DIETARY SUPPLEMENTS

Grit is an essential dietary supplement. Seed-eating birds, such as the budgerigar, need the grit to help in the digestion of food in the gizzard. Those deprived of grit will desperately peck at the mortar between bricks and tiles. Although it may not be ideal from a hygienic point of view it does no harm if budgerigars peck at the sandpapers that line their cages. The glues used are non-poisonous and the only danger is if they begin to eat the backing paper.

CUTTLEFISH 'BONE'

Cuttlefish 'bone' is a valuable source of calcium and is a useful tool for young budgerigars to use to trim their beaks. In addition to cuttlefish 'bone', a mineral block, specially formulated for pet animals, should be provided and firmly fixed where the budgerigars can peck at it.

DRINKING WATER

In the wild, budgerigars may have to go several days without drinking. In captivity, they may not drink every day, but water must be available and always fresh.

WATER FOR BATHING

Water is also needed for bathing. Unless a budgerigar can wet its feathers, it cannot preen properly. This is one reason why budgerigars will sit out in the rain in an aviary.

Those kept in cages must be provided with a shallow saucer of water in which they may splash. Alternatively it is possible to spray budgerigars with lukewarm water from an atomizer spray, or to provide them with damp turf to roll on. Provide water for bathing only on warm days, and always allow enough time for the bird's feathers to dry before roosting time.

FOOD HYGIENE

Budgerigars are scatter feeders, eating little and often. The food dish should be kept topped up, and once a day it must be cleared, cleaned, and filled with fresh food. Food that has gone mouldy or been polluted by flies is a source of disease. At the same time, the water should be replaced.

Seed mixes should be bought in small quantities to ensure freshness, and stored in a lidded container. The oil in seed stored for too long will go rancid.

Budgerigars should never be fed kitchen scraps or be given 'treats' such as chocolate.

Budgerigars need to wet their feathers if they are to preen properly. Provide a saucer of tepid water, or a damp turf, early on a warm day, so that the feathers will have time to dry before the temperature falls towards evening.

Opposite
Budgerigars enjoy millet, which can be bought either as a complete spray or compacted into a solid cake for them to peck.

Hygiene

Budgerigars groom themselves, and do not need any help from their owners. But time does need to be set aside for the cleaning of the living quarters.

DAILY ATTENTION
Each day will produce quite a litter of droppings, seed husks, uneaten greenstuff and, in the moulting season, feathers, and these should be removed daily. This chore is made much easier if sanded paper is used for the cage bottom.

Every day, after the free flight period, check the room furniture, surfaces and floors for droppings. These are easily removed using a paper towel, and will not stain.

WEEKLY CLEANING
At least once a week the cage needs a more thorough cleaning. It is convenient to do this while the budgerigar is exercising outside. Remove all the cage furniture and wash it. Check toys for cracks or sharp edges, and remove anything that is damaged. Use a damp cloth or paper towel to wipe over the cage itself, including the perches. Check that perches have not been worn smooth. If they have, roughen them slightly with coarse sandpaper.

CLEANING AVIARIES
Aviaries demand a more ambitious cleaning programme. Uneaten food and empty husks should be removed daily, together with any piles of droppings under the perches. The sleeping quarters should be checked and any droppings, feathers or other rubbish removed.

Weekly, the floor of the aviary should be washed down if it is a hard standing. If not, the more obvious rubbish should be removed and the surface raked over. Toys and other items of furniture should be cleaned and checked, and this is a good opportunity to check the general condition of the aviary. Pay particular attention to weatherproofing, the condition of the wire mesh, and any signs of rats.

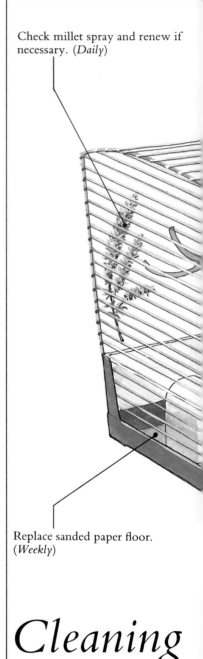

Check millet spray and renew if necessary. (*Daily*)

Replace sanded paper floor. (*Weekly*)

Cleaning Checklist

Remove and wash cage toys. (*Weekly*)

Wipe over cage with damp cloth or paper towel. (*Weekly*)

Remove perches, clean and roughen if worn smooth. (*Weekly*)

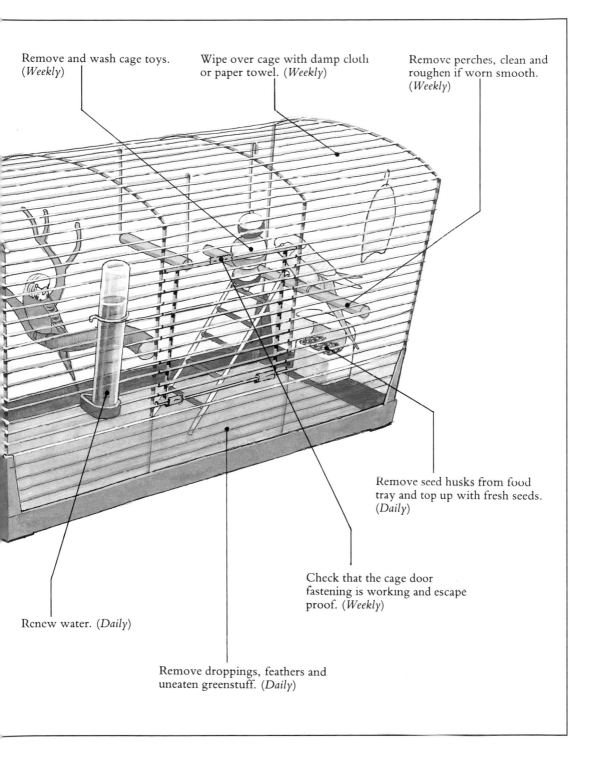

Remove seed husks from food tray and top up with fresh seeds. (*Daily*)

Check that the cage door fastening is working and escape proof. (*Weekly*)

Renew water. (*Daily*)

Remove droppings, feathers and uneaten greenstuff. (*Daily*)

Handling and training

The key to the successful handling and training of a budgerigar is to make this the responsibility of an individual member of the family. Generally, birds respond best to the pitch of a female or a child's voice, and cocks respond more readily than hens. All handling and training is best done with no one else in the room, and no distractions from, for example, radio or television.

Budgerigars can be handled quite frequently without stress, but a newly acquired bird should be allowed to settle for a day or so in its new home before being approached.

BONDING

A single budgerigar will bond to its owner and regard him or her as another member of its flock. The bond is strengthened by regular attention – conversation, training and handling sessions, and company in general. If the bird has to be left on its own for periods during the day it can benefit from a radio talk programme at fairly low volume.

FINGER-TAMING

Finger-taming is the first stage in successful handling, and it should first be tried out in the cage. The index finger should be offered through the cage door as a perch. All movements should be slow but deliberate, and the hand must be kept below the level of the bird's head. Many birds will instinctively hop on to the finger, especially if encouraged with a few softly spoken words.

An alternative is to hold out a piece of wood as a perch, which some birds will accept more readily. If this is successful, you can try with the finger later. Either way, the exercise should be repeated until the bird automatically accepts the invitation. Once the bird responds confidently within the cage, it may be taken outside.

Finger-taming is important as a means of returning a bird to its cage after its free flight period. Catching a bird that will not come to the finger may turn into an exhausting and, for the bird, possibly alarming chase.

Budgerigars should also be accustomed to being held with one hand gently over its back as shown in the illustration. The tail should lie along the inside of the wrist, and the head should rest between the first and second fingers. The thumb and the other fingers can then restrain the wings so that they cannot be fluttered and broken. Once the bird is in position, make a conscious effort to relax the fingers so that the grip is not too tight.

In an emergency, a budgerigar may be caught by dropping a duster over it and picking it up carefully.

If it is necessary to take the bird to the vet, it should if possible travel in its cage. Failing that, use a secure box with airholes – suitable cardboard containers can be obtained from pet shops.

TALKING

Training a budgerigar to talk must start when it is five or six weeks old. It calls for patience and persistence, and can be a frustrating business. Some budgerigars simply never learn to talk, however skilled and patient the trainer.

Training should take place with no other distractions in the room. If the bird is finger-tame it can be spoken to directly and give the trainer its full attention.

Eyeball-to-eyeball teaching is the key to training a budgerigar to talk.

The first word to be taught is the bird's name, which should be chosen for its short, distinctive sound. One word or, later, a short sentence should be taught at a time. The budgerigar learns to imitate exactly what it hears, and for this reason consistency is essential. The word must always be said with the same accent and inflection. The bird will need to hear the word over and over again, and may not imitate it immediately. As when a young child learns to speak, one may suddenly hear a new word being tried out long after it was last spoken.

Well-trained budgerigars can build up a considerable repertoire of words and sentences. Particularly good mimics may copy other sounds they hear about the house, such as the ring of the telephone, and may pick up words from people other than their 'official' trainer. Many birds – including some that will not talk – can be taught to whistle tunes.

PLAYING GAMES

Budgerigars can also be taught to play games with swings, ladders and other toys. The appropriate actions should be demonstrated with the finger, at the same time giving a command like 'Have a swing' or 'Ring the bell'.

Handling and training sessions should not be allowed to go on for too long, or the budgerigar will become bored. Ten or fifteen minutes is about right, but another session can follow an hour or so later.

The best conditions for pet budgerigars combine companionship and freedom.

The healthy budgerigar

Budgerigars are among the hardiest of birds when kept in clean, dry surroundings, and fed good quality food. They do, however, lose condition fast when they fall ill, so get to know your birds well and you will quickly recognize any change in them. The main signs of health are as follows:

Abdomen	the smooth outline of the bird should be unbroken by hollows, pads of fat, or growths.
Appetite	feeds mostly early morning: dehusks seed with beak and eats only kernels.
Beak	neither undershot nor overshot; able to dehusk seed. Gasping with beak open is a sign of fever or laboured breathing.
Breathing	quiet and rapid, with beak closed.
Cere	waxy in appearance, with no encrustation. After first moult at about 12 weeks the adult colour shows: blue (male); brown (female).
Claws and feet	no malformation; no encrustation; no overgrown claws.
Demeanour	normally quiet and approachable with periods of activity. Alert, observant, imitative and acrobatic.
Droppings	firm; quick to harden.
Eyes	bright and watchful; no discharge; third eyelid not showing.
Feathers	luxuriant, with none missing (except at times of moult); well-preened and held close to body except when fluffed out in cold spells or in ill health. A good sheen is natural; spiky head feathers a sign of illness.
Forehead	bar-headed birds, with striations across the forehead, are young birds not yet flighted.
Stance	sits well clear of the perch, at an angle of 30° from the upright; no hunching or huddling; no loss of balance.
Tail	the long tail feathers are lost twice a year during autumn and spring.
Vent	clean with no staining or scouring.
Wings	strong, well-feathered, able to support the budgerigar easily in flight.

Health problems can be made less likely by taking care with the siting of the budgerigar's living quarters. The ideal site in the house for the bird's cage is one where the temperature is most constant. This rules out the kitchen, for example, where there are usually extremes of heat and cold through the day and night. Other unsuitable sites include bay windows, which are cold at night and probably draughty, and passageways. In most households the best answer is to place the cage in the living-room away from windows and doorways, with a light cloth to cover the cage at night.

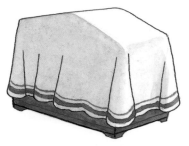

A light cloth cover provides darkness and extra protection from draughts at night or when travelling.

EXERCISE

A budgerigar should not be kept unless it is able to exercise daily in free flight. Provided there is no possibility of the bird escaping or coming to harm from dangerous equipment or other pets, it should be allowed as much freedom as possible. If there are children in the house, it is wise to arrange free flight sessions at the same fixed time each day so that doors or windows are not inadvertently opened.

If its cage is large enough, the budgerigar will also obtain some flying exercise there. For this reason, there should not be too many toys or other obstructions. It is better to have a few toys at a time and change them frequently.

LEAVING YOUR PET

As budgerigars need company and also because it is essential to top up and remove the husks from their food supply at frequent intervals, they are unsuitable pets – at any rate as cage-birds – if they have to be left alone for long periods during the day. If an emergency arises, or when you are away on holiday, arrangements should be made for a friend or neighbour either to look in and feed the bird, or to give it a temporary home. Starvation is a fairly common cause of death in budgerigars.

GOING ON HOLIDAY

If a family is going on holiday in self-catering accommodation, there is no reason why the budgerigar should not be taken along. It can travel in its own cage with a cloth covering, which will encourage it to sleep during the journey. Budgerigars are prone to heat exhaustion which may be brought on by conditions in a car on a long journey in summer. Keep the cage out of direct sunlight and dampen the cover of the cage – a plant spray full of water can be taken to renew the dampness during the journey.

First aid

It is not difficult to see when a budgerigar is unwell. Typical symptoms include untidy feathers, except during the annual moult, a puffed up or ragged appearance, and a hunched stance. A sick bird may appear sleepy, take little interest in its environment, inside or outside the cage, and give up eating. The vent may become soiled from scouring, and the droppings streaked with blood. Very often the breathing will be affected (see p.36: Colds, bronchitis and pneumonia).

As with most animals, symptoms set in very quickly, which emphasizes the importance of a daily inspection of birds during play and training sessions. In general, treatment at home is not advisable. If a budgerigar shows signs of sickness, the best thing to do is to contact a vet, and in the meantime make sure that the bird is kept warm, using a cover for the cage if necessary and keeping the bird as quiet and comfortable as possible. If you have more than one bird, the sick one should be isolated.

Many health problems can easily be solved by the vet. For example, a budgerigar with an overgrown beak will not be able to pick up enough food and will rapidly decline. If the beak is clipped by the vet, the bird will begin to eat again and recover within a day or so.

Eyes dull and uninterested

Hunched back

Head drooping

Cere encrusted

Breathing with beak open

Fat on abdomen

Feathers spiky or untidy (except during moult)

Claws malformed or unable to grip perch easily

SYMPTOMS OF POOR HEALTH

Ailments

It is very difficult for an owner to diagnose illness in a budgerigar because the same symptoms, such as a greenish diarrhoea, appear in more than one complaint, including psittacosis. This, and the fact that budgerigars lose condition very quickly when ill, makes it imperative to take prompt veterinary advice.

SCALY FACE
A grey encrustation that gradually spreads around the beak, cere, eyes, feet and legs is known as scaly face. It is caused by a minute organism that can be killed off by several applications of a germicidal solution or cream, available on veterinary prescription, or in proprietary form at pet accessory stores and counters.

Scaly face is contagious, and an affected bird must be isolated from all others.

Scaly face with encrustation showing around eyes and cere.

OVERGROWN BEAK
Budgerigars, and in particular young budgerigars, will trim their own beaks on a cuttlefish 'bone', which is also a valuable source of calcium. Sometimes this is not enough to prevent overgrowth, and then regular trimming by a veterinary surgeon will be necessary to control the condition which otherwise will eventually prevent a budgerigar from eating at all.

Cuttlefish 'bone' is used for beak trimming and as a source of calcium.

COLDS, BRONCHITIS AND PNEUMONIA
A budgerigar with a mild respiratory disorder may quickly respond to warmth. If the condition persists, or deteriorates, the bird will need drugs available on veterinary prescription, and any delay in seeking veterinary help may prove fatal.

The advanced symptoms are distressing: the bird sits huddled on its perch, wheezing and gasping for breath with an open beak, and often jerking the tail in a pumping action. Eventually a very sick bird will become too weak even to cling to its own perch.

RED MITES

Red mites are a greyish colour during the day; they take on the red colouring after feeding on their host bird during the night. The mites, which trouble budgerigars less than they trouble canaries, hide in cracks and crevices during the day and are almost invisible. Hygiene is vital here, and only the most rigorous cleaning, including total immersion of the cage, will eradicate an infestation.

OVERGROWN CLAWS

Sometimes a budgerigar's claws become so overgrown that they need cutting. This is a job for the vet as for some birds this procedure causes great stress. Nevertheless, it has to be done from time to time, though the frequency varies with individual birds.

The necessity for frequent clipping can be alleviated to some extent by providing perches of fruit tree twigs and roughening perches made of machined wood.

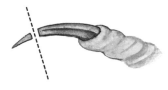

A straight cut with clippers removes the overgrown tip.

FEATHER PLUCKING

Budgerigars will sometimes peck and preen their own feathers excessively, due to boredom. The habit, once established, is difficult to stop. The introduction of a mirror, play-objects, or another budgerigar can often be sufficient distraction.

TUMOURS

Growths on or under the skin are common, and have many differing causes. Veterinary advice should be sought in the early stages, since successful treatment is frequently possible.

REGURGITATION

The regurgitation of food by healthy budgerigars should not be mistaken for vomiting. In the absence of a mate, or of young, a budgerigar in breeding condition will regurgitate food over a favourite object in its cage, or over its own feet.

PSITTACOSIS

This is the most serious disease of the parrot family. It is particularly dangerous because it can be transmitted to humans and may sometimes be fatal if not treated early enough. Pet birds, unless acquired from infected stock, are unlikely to contract it.

Reproduction

BREEDING CONDITION

Mature budgerigars are likely to reach breeding condition at any time between early spring and early autumn and sometimes during the winter too. For novice owners, it is important that the budgerigars should only be provided with nest boxes during the spring and summer, when the young chicks will have the best conditions for development.

A cock bird in breeding condition has a very bright blue cere, and a very confident manner. He will pay attention to the hen, and very likely feed her regurgitated food as if she were already incubating her eggs. A hen bird in breeding condition may also regurgitate food, as if for her chicks, and will begin to search for a nesting place. It should go without saying that only the best specimens without defects should be allowed to breed.

CLUTCH SIZE

The normal clutch consists of five or six eggs, with perhaps as many as eight in the first clutch of the year. A good pair of birds may raise three clutches a year, but both hen and cock can become exhausted by the demands of excessive breeding and will produce successively weaker broods. Unfortunately, it is sometimes the young produced by excessive breeding that find their way to the lower end of the pet market.

Responsible breeders control breeding by separating the breeding pair, removing the nesting box or removing eggs as they are laid.

EGG LAYING AND INCUBATION

The hen lays her eggs on alternate days and begins to incubate them from the time the first is laid. For this reason the chicks hatch at intervals after 18 days' incubation.

The hen will hardly leave the nest box during the incubation time, relying on the cock to feed her regurgitated seed. When they hatch, the young in turn will be fed by the hen

Pair of budgerigars with their clutch of six young who will not be ready to leave the nest box until they are at least four weeks old. They will then need to spend a further two weeks with their parents, until the first difficult task of learning to dehusk seed has been learned.

on regurgitated food and a rich 'crop-milk' that has a high protein content.

The young need no hard food provided for them until they leave the nest and begin to feed on normal mixtures. It is vital for the owner to check that the chicks are capable of feeding independently before they are removed from the parents. If they have not made the move to independence, they will starve if taken away too soon.

PAIRING

Although many budgerigars are ready for breeding at the age of three to four months, they are too immature for the strain of rearing before ten to eleven months old.

A pair normally housed together will usually rear several broods a year, if they are allowed the facilities. In aviaries the birds will pair up by choice, and great care must be taken to see that there are equal numbers of cocks and hens.

Extra nest boxes need to be provided, or there will be much squabbling over possession of the most favoured boxes, which are invariably the highest.

Nest boxes and breeding cages

Budgerigars do not build nests in Australia, nor will they in captivity. In the wild the birds lay their eggs in the hollows of gnarled eucalyptus shrubs, and make no attempt to line the holes, even with plucked feathers.

In captivity budgerigars must be provided with a nesting box, such as the one illustrated here, fitted to the side of a breeding cage. In an aviary there must be a box for each pair of birds, with extra boxes to allow the budgerigars some freedom of choice, and to forestall squabbling.

The depression in the base will hold the eggs, and there is no need to line it or soften it in any way. Essentials are that the nesting box has a small round opening for the hen to use, with a perch beneath it. The cock bird will normally use this perch to feed her while the chicks are in the nest.

The front of the nesting box is fitted with a glass screen behind the wooden door. This allows the interior of the box to be inspected, and the progress of the nestlings noted, without disturbing them or causing them to become chilled.

Droppings accumulate in the nest box very quickly during the month or more the young are developing there. If necessary, it is possible to put the nestlings into a cardboard box temporarily, and remove them to a warm place for a short time while the nest box is being cleaned. This

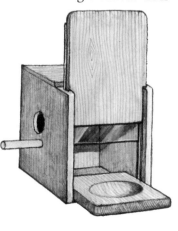

Nesting box opened up to show interior. The saucer-shaped depression serves as a nest. Budgerigars in the wild lay their eggs in hollow trees.

It is a mistake for beginners to provide nest boxes too early in the year. The best time for novice keepers to try to breed their budgerigars is from mid-spring to midsummer.

should not be done before the chicks are two weeks old. A dry scraper and kitchen towels should be used to remove the mess, and the nesting box should be kept dry. This procedure also enables the owner to check the condition of the chicks. It may be found that some have droppings caked on their claws or beaks. These may be removed using a kitchen towel dipped in lukewarm water.

CAGE DESIGN

Professional budgerigar breeders favour breeding cages of this design, which are stackable and easy to construct.

The design can be recommended just as well for budgerigars that are not breeding. Its simplicity, protection from draughts, and spaciousness are features that many expensive manufactured cages lack.

The cages may be constructed of timber or hardboard, and the wire fronts constructed of weldmesh or wiremesh. Fronts such as the one in the illustration may be bought separately, and fitted to slide into position, or fixed with a separate entrance door for the birds.

FURNISHINGS

The breeding cage does not need furnishing with mirrors or play-objects while a pair of budgerigars is rearing a brood. Boredom is not then a problem, since both cock and hen have a positive role to play. At other times of the year, birds kept in a cage of this design will need it furnished as outlined on p.24.

NEST BOX

The nest box must not be fixed into position until the birds are in breeding condition (p.38) and the time of year favourable. Without a nest box this cage provides good accommodation for a pair of birds throughout the year.

SIZE

Recommended size for the breeding cage is at least 91 × 45 × 45 cm/36 × 18 × 18 in.

The young

The chicks spend at least the first four weeks of life in the nest box, tended by both cock and hen, who are devoted in their care of the young.

There are recorded instances of either the cock or the hen dying during the time their young were still in the nest, and yet the surviving parent succeeded in rearing the entire brood. It also happens that if there is a spare hen in a colony of budgerigars, one of the cocks will raise two families, feeding both the hens concerned.

When the chicks hatch they are blind and naked, but by the end of the first week their eyes are open and their feathers beginning to grow. At four weeks they are fully feathered, and will soon be sufficiently mature to leave the protection of the nest.

At this age they need some help in making the transition to hard food, for they find it difficult at first to dehusk the seed. Again the cock helps them, until at six weeks they are fully fledged, able to care for themselves, and ready to be rehomed if necessary. These very young budgerigars have dark horizontal markings across the forehead, which disappear after the first moult at about twelve weeks.

Sexing the young birds is not as easy as sexing adult budgerigars. In good health, adult cocks have a blue or violet cere; adult females have a mushroom brown cere. In many juveniles these colours are not yet distinct and sexing the young becomes a matter of guesswork. This accounts for the fact that many people have given a home to a Joey, only to find later on that she has to be renamed.

Finding homes for budgerigars is not usually so difficult a task as finding homes for many other animals, but it is sensible to allow a breeding pair to raise only a limited number of chicks in a season. This is not only a matter of re-homing: both cock and hen become exhausted by raising their young, and they should not be expected to raise more than six to eight chicks a year.

The chicks should not be rehomed singly. These are flock birds and a lone budgerigar is never seen in nature.

At six to ten weeks, these budgerigar chicks will be fully fledged and ready to be rehomed. They will moult at about twelve weeks, when the bars across their foreheads will disappear. By this time, males and females should be separated.

Your questions answered

My budgerigar won't take a bath. How can I encourage him?

Male budgerigars in particular are sometimes reluctant to bath. However, bathing and subsequent preening are important social as well as hygienic activities and should be encouraged. One way is to put a favourite titbit such as a small piece of lettuce or carrot in the water so that in order to retrieve it the bird must get slightly wet and will then preen itself. Alternatively, use a house plant spray on a 'mist' setting, aiming to let the mist fall rather than squirting it directly. It is always important not to overdo it and to allow time for the feathers to dry before roosting for the night.

As I have been told that a budgerigar kept alone gets very bored, we bought two males as company for each other. All they seem to do is to peck at their own and each other's feathers. What is wrong?

Gentle pecking which does not leave feathers flying is just a sign of companionship. But rougher treatment, perhaps drawing blood, may well be a sign of overcrowding. Here is a check list of points for you. Is the cage large enough? If they peck at each other, they may not have enough personal space. Do the birds have a period of free flight every day? This is essential for health and contentment. Do you spend enough time talking to your birds and playing with them? Plenty of human contact is vital. Have you provided an interesting range of toys, changed frequently? Is there a variety of perches in the cage?

Will keeping a budgerigar affect my child's asthma?

You should take a doctor's advice before buying a bird. Asthma is unpredictable in its side-effects, but problems are not inevitable. It would be wise to delegate cleaning the cage to someone else to avoid contact with feather fragments and dust, and of course no budgerigar should be kept in a bedroom, whether the owner is asthmatic or not.

I have recently acquired an aviary which I am in the process of stocking. Are there any special precautions I should take in case of a severe winter?
As a general precaution, check that the sleeping quarters are draughtproof, especially at corners and at the wall and roof joints. The aviary should be sited where it gets morning or afternoon sun, if possible with some nearby protection, such as shrubs or a fence, from the worst weather. The birds should, of course, be shut in their quarters at night. Take care that the aviary is ratproof; it will be particularly tempting to rats if the weather is cold.

My budgerigar always gnaws his sandsheet unless I entice him with a stick of millet. Is there a limit to how much millet he should have?
There is no restriction on millet, but it sounds as if your bird's problem is a lack of grit in the diet. Grit is essential as it is stored in the gizzard and used to digest food. A small container of grit should be available at all times. Check and, if necessary, renew it daily.

I would like to give my elderly mother a budgerigar for her birthday, but I am not sure whether giving pets as presents is a good idea.
Giving pets as presents should always be approached with caution. Sound out your mother first and find out whether she would welcome a budgerigar. Ensure that, if you give her one, it comes with all the equipment and initial food, grit and so on that she will need, and that she has a copy of this book. It is not a good idea to introduce a pet to a new home at festive times when there may be unusual noise and excitement and routines may be upset. Having said all this, budgerigars do make excellent, companionable and relatively undemanding pets for elderly people.

Can owners catch psittacosis from budgerigars?
Psittacosis is a disease of members of the parrot family with symptoms similar to typhoid. It can be communicated to human beings. It is not endemic in budgerigars but occurs in sporadic and often widespread outbreaks. Cases of psittacosis in humans are occasionally reported, but the risk of catching the disease is generally low. Any unexpected respiratory problems should naturally be checked out by your doctor. At all times, sensible hygiene precautions should be taken

Life history

Scientific name	*Melopsittacus undulatus*
Incubation period	18 days
Clutch size	3-10
Birth weight	2 g
Eyes open	6 days
Plumage complete	28 days
Leave nest	28 days (approx.)
Fully fledged	5-6 weeks
Puberty	3-4 months
Adult weight	35 g/1 oz-60 g/2 oz
Best age to breed	males 10+ months females 11+ months
Breeding season	early spring to autumn
Retire from breeding	males 6 years females 4 years
Life expectancy	5-10 years

Record card

Record sheet for your own budgerigars

(photograph or portrait)

(photograph or portrait)

Name

Date of birth
(actual or estimated)

Sex

Colour/description

Name

Date of birth
(actual or estimated)

Sex

Colour/description

Feeding notes

Medical notes

Veterinary surgeon's name

Practice address

Surgery hours

Tel. no.

Index